IMAGES
of Aviation

SAUNDERS ROE

Samuel Edgar Saunders, the founder of the Company was born at the Swan Inn, Streatley-on-Thames in 1857, and died at Nettlestone on the Isle of Wight in 1933 at the age of 76. He had a reputation for being a gifted engineer and a generous and kind hearted gentleman.

IMAGES
of Aviation

SAUNDERS ROE

Compiled by
Raymond L. Wheeler RDI

TEMPUS

First published 1998, reprinted 1999
Copyright © Raymond L. Wheeler RDI, 1998

Tempus Publishing Limited
The Mill, Brimscombe Port,
Stroud, Gloucestershire, GL5 2QG

Arcadia Publishing
2 Cumberland Street
Charlston, SC 29401

ISBN 0 7524 1075 X

Typesetting and origination by
Tempus Publishing Limited
Printed in Great Britain by
Midway Clark Printing, Wiltshire

Dedicated to the memory of
Samuel Edgar Saunders and Sir Alliott Verdon Roe

Contents

The Swan Inn at Streatley on the River Thames where Samuel Edgar Saunders was born in 1857. In the foreground is the steam launch *Flying Dutchman*, which was claimed to be the fastest boat on the Thames, at 17.4 mph, when it was built in 1876. She was later renamed *Lorna Doone*.

Introduction

Samuel Edgar Saunders, the Saunders of Saunders Roe, was born in 1857 at the Swan Inn at Streatley-on-Thames. His father Cornelius and mother Eleanor lived there with Samuel's grandfather Moses, who was responsible for the construction of the local weir and associated locks from 1830. He was also the ferryman as no bridge across the weir then existed. Without doubt the family made their own boats, and Samuel is reputed to have made his own dinghy when a young boy. Apparently the villagers were so proud of his skill that the boat was paraded round the village for all to see and admire.

Advertisements in the local papers and magazines of the 1890s show that an S.E. Saunders Company was founded in 1870 when Samuel was only 13! Perhaps the Company was set up for him by his parents and grandparents in anticipation of his future career. Certainly by the 1880s the Company was prospering, and had already gained a reputation for very high quality workmanship and pretty designs. To support his expanding business new buildings sprang up around the inn, across the river at Goring and near South Stoke, some one and a half miles up river from Goring.

With the advent of the Daimler internal combustion engine in the 1880s Sam saw an opportunity to expand his business. He realised that a new method of lightweight hull construction would be needed to take full advantage of this engine which was so much lighter than the current steam engines. He devised and patented a laminated monocoque form of construction formed of thin layers of diagonal and longitudinal planking sewn together with copper wire or annealed brass. He clearly had no faith in glues of the day. Waterproofing was provided by interlayers of fine canvas cloth impregnated with boiled linseed oil. The copper stitches were 1 inch long and in rows 1 inch apart. He named his new method of construction Consuta, Latin for 'sewn together'. It is not too far fetched to regard this invention as a composite material and it is intriguing to note that the present Company, GKN Westland Aerospace Limited, depends on high technology composite construction as the main part of its business. The first boat to utilize the Consuta method was a launch built for Henley Regatta umpires in 1896. Also called *Consuta*, this launch was subsequently used until the late 1960s by the BBC to follow the Oxford and Cambridge boat race - clearly a tribute to Samuel Saunders and his staffs' workmanship and the soundness of his Consuta invention. The *Consuta* still exists at a boat yard in Chertsey. The launch also embodied Sam's ideas on hydrodynamic hull design as she had a fine entry, a long shallow run aft with a rounded tunnel stern which gave her a speed of 27 knots with a negligible wash. The public success of *Consuta* soon brought considerable business to the Company.

In 1899 Sam Saunders and four of his senior staff decided to form a new company which they called the Saunders Patent Launch Building Syndicate. With the death of Queen Victoria in 1901 and the accession of Edward VII, yachting and boating on the Solent, especially at Cowes, expanded rapidly. Export business was also expanding and transporting boats from the Thames had its difficulties. Thus the Syndicate decided to move to Cowes in 1901, and began work in Alexandra Hall adjacent to the River Medina at West Cowes. All was well until 1906 when, for reasons unknown, Sam decided to break away from the Syndicate and take over the almost derelict works of the Liquid Fuel Engineering Company at East Cowes. This site, still known as Columbine Yard, remains the main home of the successive companies which have inherited the Sam Saunders' entrepreneurial spirit. He was awarded the unusual distinction of being made a Chevalier of the Order of St Charles of Monaco for his contributions to Monaco Regattas.

The other pioneer whose name appears in the title of this book was Alliott Verdon Roe, who was born at Patricroft, near Manchester, in 1877. He served an apprenticeship in locomotive engineering and obtained a degree in marine engineering at King's College, London University. The aircraft bug soon took possession of him and in 1907 he won a competition for model aircraft organised by the *Daily Mail*. The same year he designed, built and flew his first aeroplane, the first Englishman to do so. With his brother Humphrey he formed A.V. Roe and Company in 1910, producing the famous Avro 504 bomber in 1913.

By a fortunate coincidence, when Sam Saunders at the age of 71 decided to sell his Company in 1928, Alliott Verdon Roe had also decided to sell his Avro Company and was thus able to buy a controlling interest in S.E. Saunders Limited. In 1929 the new board, with Sam as President and Sir Alliott as Chairman, agreed to rename the Company Saunders Roe Limited. Alliott Verdon Roe was knighted in 1929 for his services to aviation. He was elected President of the Company on the death of Sam in 1933, a position he retained until his own death in 1958.

In 1959 the Company was purchased by Westland Aircraft Limited and it

The Oxford University boat club barge built by Saunders in 1878, which has been recently completely restored by the Thames and Kennet Marina Company who make it available for hire.

The Springfield Works of Sam Saunders at South Stoke on the north side of the River Thames, some one and a half miles upstream of Goring-on-Thames. This photograph was taken in the mid 1890s.

was known as their Saunders Roe Division. Then in 1966, with hovercraft business booming, the British Hovercraft Corporation was formed in combination with the Vickers Supermarine and the National Research and Development Corporation hovercraft interests.

Later, in 1985 when the Westland Group encountered financial difficulties and was restructured, the East Cowes operation became Westland Aerospace Limited. The latest takeover occurred in 1994 when Westland was acquired by GKN, and Westland Aerospace retained its name. Since then the Company has prospered and doubled in size.

Products for which the Company made notable contributions to new technology were flying boats, fighter aircraft, amphibians and space launchers. Boats have included fast displacement vessels, world record hydroplanes, *Miss England II* and *Bluebird K3*, motor yachts, hydrofoils and hovercraft. More detailed contributions include computing, load monitoring, radar aerials, army pontoons, specialised plywoods and structural and hydrodynamic research.

It is a great tribute to the example of expertise, hard work and dedication to quality set by Sam Saunders, Sir Alliott Verdon Roe and the other entrepreneurs who followed them that the Company has survived and thrived despite world wars, economic recessions, acquisitions and the continuous, rapid development of technology.

Boat construction in progress at Springfield Works at the end of the 1890s.

Running at 27½ miles an hour.

The first launch built of laminated wood sewn together with copper wire was called *Consuta* after the name given to the patented method of construction. She was built as the umpires' launch for the Leander Club at Henley-on-Thames and was subsequently used for many years for the same purpose for the Oxford and Cambridge boat race.

The interior of *Consuta's* hull, clearly showing the method of construction and the copper stitching.

Consuta, and her sister ship, *Maritana*, as escort, acting as the umpires' launch in the 1912 Oxford and Cambridge boat race.

The steam launch *Victoria* was built around 1906 by the Saunders Syndicate at Springfield Works. She was originally built as a day hire motor launch called *Rosetta*. Her hull is of Consuta laminated construction and she has been completely restored by Mr and Mrs Ian Rutter.

The Saunders Syndicate's first premises at Cowes, Isle of Wight, were at Alexandra Hall in Birmingham Road. This photograph was taken at the rear of the premises in around 1904. The hall still exists as a private residence.

The premises at East Cowes called Columbine Yard, in 1897, which were said to be almost derelict when taken over by Sam Saunders in 1906.

Columbine Yard in 1910, showing a new or refurbished shed on the site. To the right, in the background, is the White House which was Sam Saunders' home for many years.

One

S.E. Saunders Limited
1906-1929

The first report that Samuel Saunders had moved his workforce to East Cowes appeared in the magazines Motor Boat and The Yachtsman in October 1906. Then in December 1906 it was reported that the Columbine Works of the Liquid Fuel Engineering Company at East Cowes had been refurbished, with new modern electrical machinery installed throughout. The first board meeting of the new operation took place on 16 May 1908 when the Company was named S.E. Saunders Limited. There were only two directors - Samuel and his son Hubert. Considerable financial assistance to the new Company was given by the Wolseley Tool and Motor Car Company Limited. This support continued until the advent of the First World War when the Company had so much aircraft manufacturing work that finance was not required. Following the end of the First World War, finance again became a necessity and was provided by Vickers, owners of the Wolseley Company, and they effectively took over the Company. However, business must have quickly become profitable as Sam Saunders was able to buy back all the Vickers shares in 1921. In 1909 Sam formally announced that he had formed a new department to design and build 'everything required for aero-navigation'.

The esteem and affection which his workforce felt for Sam Saunders was clearly shown when he and his wife Kate celebrated their golden wedding in 1928. A huge party was held in one of the factory buildings with over 400 employees present. The next day a sumptuous party was given for 350 old folk of the town. Following that, 600 children were entertained at a special party. It was clear from the speeches recorded in the Isle of Wight County Press that Sam Saunders was a well liked and highly respected man.

Sam Saunders and his wife Kate outside the White House, *c.* 1913. It was at this time he was created a Chevalier of the Order of St Charles of Monaco.

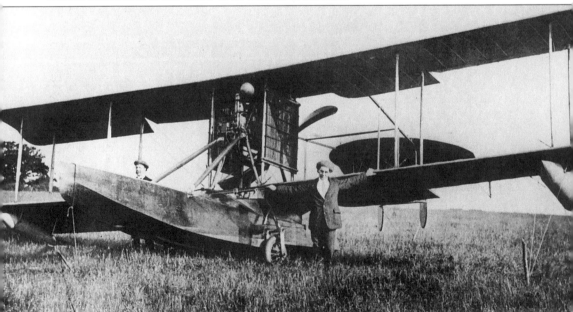

The Sopwith Bat Boat amphibian which H.G. Hawker flew in 1913 to win the Mortimer Singer Prize for seven successive landings on land and sea. The hull was constructed of Saunders lightweight Consuta laminated mahogany.

Lightweight aircraft hangars erected on the east bank of the River Medina for a primitive small airfield in 1909. In this picture the Sopwith Bat Boat is being launched in 1913. The two sheds were destroyed in a gale in 1914.

Ursula, powered by two 360 hp Wolseley engines, achieved a top speed of 44 mph in 1910. Her 50 ft long hull lines were a superb compromise between displacement and planing lines.

Consuta hull construction. Here we see one completed diagonal mahogany lamination and a workman tacking in place the fine canvas interlayer.

The Duke of Westminster's *Pioneer*, one of the first Saunders planing hulls with five steps based on the patented ideas of Fauber. This photograph, taken in Cowes harbour in 1910, shows the hull bottom of the craft after it had been recovered following a capsize. No one was injured in the accident.

Maple Leaf IV. This 40 ft long craft powered by two 400 hp special Austin engines won the Harmsworth Trophy (later renamed the British International Trophy) in 1912 and 1913. With five steps, similar to *Pioneer*, she achieved 57.5 mph (49.9 knots) driven by Tommy Sopwith, the famous pioneer aviator.

This attractive 55 ft long launch was built of Consuta laminated mahogany construction in 1912. She was powered by two Thorneycroft V8 engines giving her a cruising speed of 21 knots. She had the strange name *Kootenay*.

The Ravaud Aero-Hydroplane of 1911. The hull was 20 ft long and built of laminated Consuta construction with 'wings' of 9 ft span. The hull was borne well above the the water by streamlined floats and struts. Power was supplied by a 50 hp Gnome engine which drove a pusher airscrew. The machine was intended to skim over the water but no information is available on its effectiveness. The inventor Monsieur Ravaud is shown at the controls.

This Geoffrey de Havilland BE2a two seat observation biplane was built by S.E. Saunders Ltd in 1912. The 70 hp radial Renault engine provided a maximum speed of 72 mph. The successful construction of this machine led to the aircraft production orders of the First World War. A BE2c version with floats was also built.

The Solent Works at West Cowes was built in 1916 by the Building Construction Company and F. Bevis Ltd for the manufacture of aircraft. It was destroyed by German bombers in May 1942. This photograph was taken in 1929.

The Avro 504 A/J two seat dual controlled training biplane. Between 1915 and 1917, 201 of these aircraft were built. A single 100 hp Gnome engine powered them to a maximum speed of 82 mph.

The Short 184 two seat torpedo and bomb carrying seaplane, powered by various engines of 225 to 260 hp, was suitable for operation from carrier ships. Eighty of these seaplanes were built by S.E. Saunders Ltd between 1915 and 1916.

The Curtis H4 flying boat was equipped with at least three Consuta hulls built by S.E. Saunders Ltd. Clearly the Norman Thomson NT2B was an almost identical copy of this machine. The Felixstowe flying boats owe much to Curtis design, although many important improvements were introduced.

The Norman Thomson NT2B two seat trainer flying boat was almost identical to the Curtis H4. The engine was a 200 hp Sunbeam giving a speed of 85 mph. Twenty-four aircraft were built between 1916 and 1918; the hulls were of laminated wood construction.

The Felixstowe F2A sea patrol flying boat could carry a crew of up to five. Two 360 hp Rolls Royce Eagle engines drove it at 95 mph. One hundred aircraft were built of laminated cedar and mahogany with a fabric interlayer.

The Curtis H12 flying boat was almost indistinguishable from the F2A. Spare hulls and wing tip floats were built in quantity by S.E. Saunders Ltd during the First World War.

Felixstowe F2A production in the Solent Works on the west bank of the River Medina, opposite the Columbine factory in 1916.

The Saunders TI was the first aircraft design by S.E. Saunders Ltd. This two seat military aircraft was fitted with a 150 hp Sunbeam Nubian engine. The fuselage was of wooden monocoque laminated Consuta construction and the wings were detachable. Only one aircraft was built. First flown in 1917, it continued to fly for many years.

In March 1919 work commenced on an extensive factory for the manufacture of Consuta plywood for general use including aircraft production. The factory produced plywood until it was destroyed by fire in 1960.

The Saunders Kittiwake was a six to seven passenger biplane amphibian flying boat powered by two 200 hp ABC Wasp II radial engines. She had a top speed of 110 mph but was let down by under-developed engines. The first flight took place in September 1920.

The Vickers-Saunders Valentia BS1 was assembled and flown from Cowes with hulls built by S.E. Saunders Ltd and wings built by the Vickers Company, which virtually owned the Saunders Company at the time. This flying boat was intended for military sea patrol and offensive operational duties. She was powered by two 650 hp Rolls Royce Condor engines. The first of three machines made its initial flight in 1921.

The Vickers-Saunders Valentia undergoing routine maintenance on the hard standing of the West Cowes Solent Works in 1923.

Vickers Viking amphibian hulls were built at S.E. Saunders Ltd in the period 1919-1921. These machines were supplied for both civil and military purposes, carrying up to four passengers in either open or closed cabins.

In 1914 the Company purchased Cornubia Yard which was used for boat building until just before the Second World War, when it was used for the manufacture of aircraft components. It was completely destroyed in May 1942 during a bombing raid on Cowes. This photograph was taken in about 1925.

A set of pretty launches in the entrance to Cornubia Yard in 1925.

This standard S.E. Saunders 5 hp inboard marine engine was produced in quantity after the First World War. Similar engines of higher horse power were also available.

One of a number of luxury motor yachts built in the 1920s. This one, called *Beryl*, was built for Lord Inverclyde in 1923. The 120 ft long yacht is shown here on the slipway ready for launch. The slipway looks untidy to say the least!

Lord Inverclyde and Sam Saunders at the launch ceremony for *Beryl* on a rather crude platform in 1923.

In the 1920s Consuta laminated wood construction was still sold in many different applications, from motor car bodies to waste paper baskets. Wolseley and Bentley car bodies were made in addition to this strange looking DFP racing car, built in 1921.

The Saunders patented flying boat hull of 1923. The idea was that a tunnel along the hull centre line would gather the bow wave and pass it through to the stern. Here it is fitted to a Felixstowe F5 in 1924. The idea demonstrated some advantages but was not considered worth the additional hull weight and cost.

The Saunders A3 Valkyrie, the first design for which Henry Knowler was largely responsible. This general purpose patrol and reconnaissance flying boat powered by three 685 hp Rolls Royce Condor engines first flew in 1927. The hull was of wooden Consuta laminated construction, one of the last to be made of wood.

The Saunders A4 Medina, a civil flying boat carrying up to ten passengers. Her two 450 hp Bristol Jupiter engines gave her a top speed of 115 mph, but performance proved unsatisfactory. She was the last flying boat built by the Company with a wooden hull. First flight was in 1927 and she was dismantled in 1929.

Between 1914 and 1937 S.E. Saunders and Saunders Roe Ltd built some 61 lifeboats for the Royal National Lifeboat Institution. This picture shows a 48 ft long Ramsgate type called *Prudential* which was built in 1925 for the Ramsgate station where she served until 1953.

Mrs Seely, wife of Major General Seely, christening the lifeboat *Princess Mary* at Cornubia Yard in 1929. This lifeboat at 61 ft long was the largest in the world at this time. She had cabin space for 60 people and could carry up to 300 in calm weather.

The S.E. Saunders lifeboat workers in the late 1920s.

Another idea of Sam Saunders was the prefabricated house shown here. A small number were built in the 1920s. This one is still used as a residence on the outskirts of Newport.

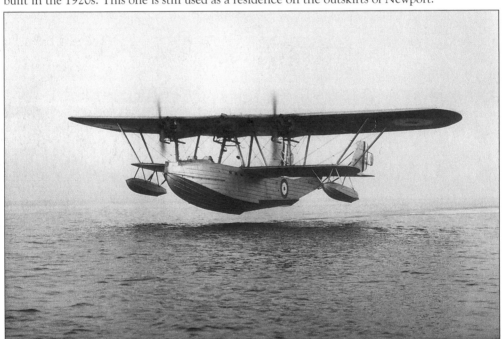

The Saunders A7 Severn general purpose military flying boat with a crew of five was S.E. Saunders' first with a metal hull. Although design commenced in 1927, the first flight was delayed by manufacturing development until 1930 - after the A.V. Roe takeover. Her three 485 hp Bristol Jupiter engines gave her a top speed of 125 mph.

The Saunders A10 fighter, more often called the Saunders Roe A10. This aircraft was designed in the S.E. Saunders era and flown in the Saunders Roe period, which commenced in December 1928. This pleasant-looking multi-gun fighter, powered by a single Rolls Royce FX1 engine, was capable of 200 mph. It first flew in 1929 and was taken over by the Aeroplane and Armament Experimental Establishment in 1931.

Columbine Yard and its associated buildings at East Cowes at the time of the takeover by Alliott Verdon Roe in 1928. Close to the prefabricated house is Seaholme House, which houses the directors of the present Company, GKN Westland Aerospace Ltd. All the buildings adjacent to the small pier were pulled down in 1935 to make way for the large hangar which is still in use by the Company.

S.E. Saunders was honoured with four royal visits by King George V and Queen Mary. On one other occasion the Queen visited him on her own to open a spacious hall for the Whippingham community where Sam lived. Here we see Sam escorting the Queen at Columbine Yard.

Two
Saunders Roe Limited
1929-1945

Samuel Saunders decided to sell his Company in 1928 at the age of 71. By a happy coincidence Alliott Verdon Roe had just sold his Avro company to J.D. Siddeley and had taken up residence at Hamble on Southampton Water. He and a colleague, John Lord, acquired a controlling interest in S.E. Saunders Limited on 23 November 1928. At the first board meeting on 12 December 1928, Sam Saunders was elected Life President, and on 9 January 1929 Alliott Verdon Roe was elected Chairman and joint Managing Director with John Lord. It was not until 27 June 1929 that the board agreed to change the name of the Company to Saunders Roe Limited. Sam's last task for his old Company whilst he was president, was to supervise the construction of Miss England II for Sir Henry Segrave, which broke the world water speed record in July 1931 at 110 mph on Lake Garda.

Whilst changes in board members took place from time to time, the main change in the Company structure before the Second World War was to create Saunders Shipyard Limited in 1937 and Saro Laminated Wood Products Limited in 1938. The change in structure was to prove significant when the Company was bought by Westland Aircraft Limited in 1959.

Alliott Verdon Roe, the first Englishman to design, build and fly his own aeroplane in 1907. He started the famous Avro aircraft company in 1910, which he sold to Armstrong Siddeley in 1928, using the proceeds to purchase a controlling interest in S.E. Saunders Ltd in the same year. The Company was renamed Saunders Roe Limited in 1929. Knighted for his service to aviation, he is shown here at a passenger door of the Princess flying boat in 1953.

The Isaaco Helicogyre helicopter built under sub-contract for research purposes. A 32 hp Bristol Cherub engine was mounted on the tip of each rotor and a 100 hp AS Genet Major engine drove a propeller for propulsion. Completed in 1929, the machine was delivered to Farnborough for testing where many problems with the power plants were experienced. It is very doubtful whether it ever flew and it was scrapped in 1932.

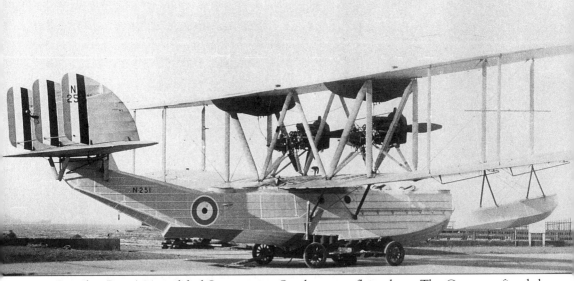

Saunders Roe A14 modified Supermarine Southampton flying boat. The Company fitted the Southampton with an aluminium alloy hull of simplified construction with corrugated external skins. Tests at Felixstowe from 1929 to 1930 showed generally favourable results, but not sufficient advantage to justify quantity production.

The Saunders A7 on trials in the Middle East in 1931. The corrugated external skin used on the A14 Southampton hull can be clearly seen. Also evident are the Commanding Officer and engineering personnel at Felixstowe, prior to departure.

The Saunders Roe A22 Segrave Meteor being prepared for engine runs at Somerton airfield. Designed as a four seat high performance civil monoplane powered by two 120 hp de Havilland Gypsy III engines, it achieved a maximum speed of 132 mph. The first flight of the only aircraft built took place in 1930 and it continued flying until 1932.

The Saunders Roe A19 Cloud amphibious flying boat was designed after a careful market study in 1928-29. This early version, which carried up to eight passengers, was powered by two 300 hp Wright Whirlwind engines, giving a maximum speed of 125 mph. Four civil versions were built after the first flight of the prototype in 1930.

The Saunders Roe A29 military Cloud. The position of the engines mounted on struts above the wing enabled a variety of engines to be installed. In all no fewer than six engine types were fitted to Clouds. Seventeen of these aircraft were delivered to the RAF for pilot and navigator training.

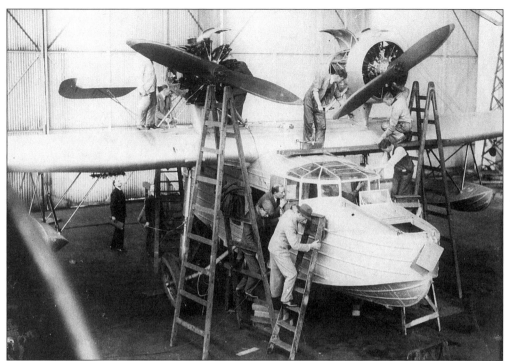

A Saro Cloud in the course of a major overhaul showing ready access to all parts of the machine. No Health and Safety restrictions in those days!

The Saunders Roe A17 Cutty Sark light four seat flying boat or amphibian for civil or military use. It was also powered by a variety of engines, in this case five. Four of the twin engines were approximately 120 hp to 140 hp, but one, the AS Lynx was of 240 hp which gave a maximum speed of 110 mph. The first machine was designed and built in the incredibly short time of five months, to have it ready for the 1929 International Aero Exhibition at Olympia.

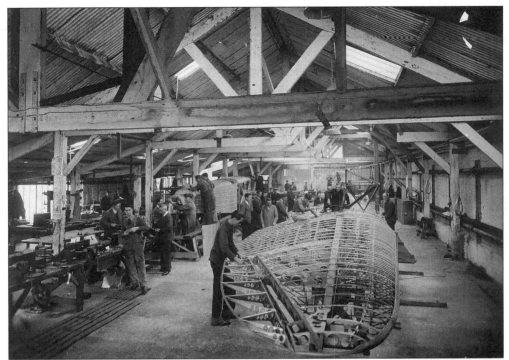

Cutty Sark wing manufacture at Folly Works on the River Medina in 1930. A total of twelve machines were built for both civil and military use.

The first of two military Cutty Sark amphibians ordered in 1932 for the Kwangsi Air Force. This machine was despatched to Hong Kong but was returned to Cowes and sold to Air Service Training for training civil flying boat pilots.

The Saro A21 Windhover was the third in this series of small early 1930s amphibious flying boats. This civil machine was designed to carry a crew of two and up to six passengers. Fitted with three 120 hp de Havilland Gypsy II engines it had a top speed of 110 mph. The first machine was launched without the small wing above the engines, which was fitted by the Australian Company Matthews Aviation. This machine first flew in 1930 and only one other was built.

A total of fifty-five Blackburn Bluebirds were built in the Cowes factory between 1929 and 1934. This aircraft was a successful two seat light biplane for club and private owner use. A variety of single engines of up to 130 hp gave them a top speed of nearly 110 mph.

Two Blackburn Bluebirds were fitted with twin seaplane floats at Cowes in 1929. After trials in the Solent this machine was despatched to Norway.

The Spartan Cruiser, designated A24 by Saunders Roe Ltd, was developed from the earlier Mailplane. Spartan Aircraft had been absorbed into the Saro Company in the early 1930s. Sixteen aircraft in three Marks were built between 1932 and 1935. Mark III, shown here, was powered by three 130 hp de Havilland Gypsy Major engines, enabling the aircraft to carry up to eight passengers 550 miles at a cruising speed of 110 mph.

One Spartan Clipper was built at Saunders Roe Ltd in 1932. This aircraft, fitted with a 75 hp Pobjoy R engine, competed in the King's Cup Air race in 1933. It was still flying in 1938 when a 90 hp Niagara III engine was installed.

The luxury motor yacht *Velda* was built in 1931 for Captain Leslie Irwin the parachute expert. Powered by twin Sterling 180 hp engines and fitted with a subsidiary schooner sailing rig, she had a cruising speed of 14 knots.

Miss England II breaking the world water speed record for the third time at 110.22 mph in July 1931 on Lake Garda, with Kay Don at the helm. She was built for Sir Henry Segrave who was killed when the craft capsized on Lake Windermere in 1930. Designed by Fred Cooper, Sam Saunders himself personally supervised her construction - his last task for the Company.

Miss England II was raised from the bottom of Lake Windermere after the accident in 1930 when she hit an object in the water at high speed and capsized. She had already broken the world water speed record at 98.76 mph in the hands of Sir Henry Segrave. The hole in her hull forward of the step can be seen in the photograph.

Sam Saunders died in 1933 aged 76. Here former employees and friends draw a special carriage with his mahogany boat-shaped coffin from outside his home at Padmore House, East Cowes. The funeral took place at St Mildred's Church, Whippingham, on 21 December.

Sir Malcolm Campbell at the helm of *Bluebird K3*, which was designed by Fred Cooper and Reid Ralton after extensive tests on four models at the Admiralty Test Tank at Haslar in 1936. She was built by Saunders Roe Ltd at East Cowes. This picture was taken at Lake Hallwyl near Geneva, where the world speed record was raised to 130.94 mph on 17 September 1938.

A model of a proposed futuristic flying boat called Pterodactyl VIII. This was a collaborative design by G.T.R. Hill of Westland Aircraft Ltd and Henry Knowler, the Chief Designer of Saunders Roe Ltd around 1937.

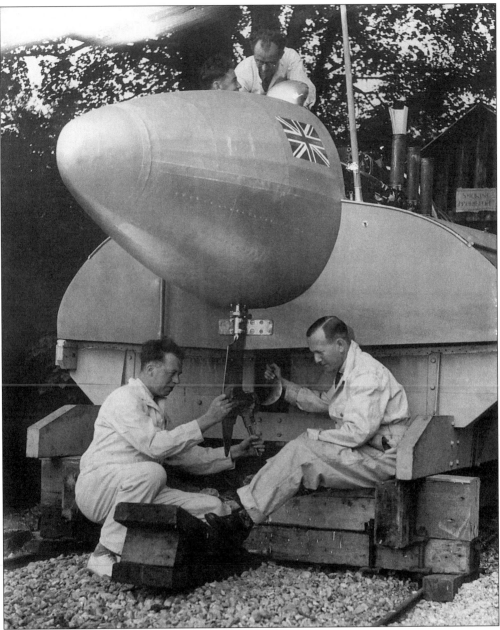

Engineers working on the stern of *Bluebird K3*. She was powered by a Rolls Royce R37 2,500 hp engine, driving a very high speed propellor rotating at some 9,000 rpm. The same engine was used to drive the Supermarine S6B when it won the Schneider Trophy for Britain.

The Saunders Roe A27 London Mark I general purpose reconnaissance flying boat with a crew of five. Two Bristol Pegasus III engines gave the aircraft a maximum speed of 145 mph. One ton of bombs could be carried under the wings. This aircraft is the prototype and was first flown in March 1934. Eleven of these popular aircraft were built for the RAF.

The Saunders Roe London Mark II, fitted with the Bristol Pegasus X 1,055 hp engine which increased the top speed to 155 mph. Twenty of these very successful machines were built for the RAF, the last being delivered in 1938.

Saro Londons in production at Columbine Yard, East Cowes, in 1937.

Saunders Roe A29 Cloud modified to test a new concept in flying boat design. The floats have been replaced by large sponsons and the wing with a new monospar design. Trials in 1935 and 1936 showed the concept to be successful.

The Saunders Roe A33 unnamed long range reconnaissance flying boat with a crew of seven, built for the RAF. Powered by four 830 hp Bristol Perseus XII engines it was expected to achieve a maximum speed of 200 mph and an endurance of twelve hours. Unfortunately a heavy landing caused a wing structural failure in 1938 and the prototype was written off.

The Saunders Roe S36 Lerwick, another high performance reconnaissance flying boat with a crew of up to seven. This one was powered by two 1,375 hp Bristol Hercules II or IV engines giving a maximum speed of 215 mph and a range of 1,500 miles. Two thousand pounds of bombs or depth charges could be carried in the engine nacelles. Twenty-one aircraft were built between 1938 and early 1941; the first flight was at the end of 1938.

Production in the Columbine hangar in 1937 shows the last of the Londons, the A33 hull on the left and the Lerwick on the right.

The Saunders Roe design department investigated a replacement of the Short C class civil passenger carrying flying boat in 1938. The proposal was that it should be significantly larger and the decision was made to build this scaled-down model. This machine, the Saro A37, was nicknamed the 'Shrimp' by the workforce! Powered by four Pobjoy Niagara III 90 hp engines it had a maximum speed of 130 mph. All hydrodynamic and aerodynamic characteristics were found to be extremely good. Designed and built in only seven months she first flew in September 1939; trials with 'Shrimp' continued until September 1947.

The demand for Spitfire production compelled Supermarine to offload the manufacture of their Walrus amphibian to Saunders Roe in 1939. The machine was required for reconnaissance, air-sea rescue and training. With a single 750 hp Bristol Pegasus VI engine it was capable of 135 mph. Mark I machines with metal hulls designed by Supermarine were supplied to five air forces, including the RAF; 270 aircraft were built by Saunders Roe. A further 191 Mark II machines with wooden hulls designed by Saunders Roe were also constructed. The photograph shows a Walrus on a catapult launcher.

The Walrus was required to operate in rough seas in order to rescue airmen and when the craft was lifted back onto the warship after a patrol. Here we see one crew member balanced on the engine nacelle ready to catch the slinging hook from the warship, and another on the starboard wing balancing the engine torque. Incredibly this was routine procedure!

Much of the Saunders Roe Walrus production was transferred to Addlestone near Weybridge in late 1941 and early 1942. This picture shows a typical example of wartime factory improvisation. Production ceased in January 1944.

After the Second World War a number of Walrus aircraft were sold to civil operators. Six were sold to United Whalers Ltd, to act as spotters from a new whale factory ship the *Balaena*. One of these flying boats, seen here, won the 1946 Folkestone Aero Trophy Race at an average speed of 121 mph.

In 1942 manufacturing commenced at Cowes, Eastleigh and Addlestone of a development of the Walrus called the Sea Otter. The first aircraft was flown in January 1943 and when production was completed in July 1946, 290 had been completed for the RAF and the Fleet Air Arm. The engine for the Sea Otter was a 965 hp Bristol Mercury XXX.

Final assembly of Sea Otters in the Columbine hangar in 1944.

During the Second World War the Saunders Roe Folly Works built these 16 ft long folding assault boats in quantity. A similar design of a two man canoe for commando operations was also in production.

The building of bridging pontoons for the British Army began at Folly Works in 1934. During the Second World War main production was taken over by Saunders Roe Shipyard Ltd, which had been transferred from East Cowes to Edmonton, North London, as shown here. After the war the shipyard was transferred to Beaumaris, on the Isle of Anglesey, where quantity production of pontoons continued into the 1950s.

Shortly after the Second World War commenced the Company design team moved to Beaumaris for the duration of the conflict. There they continued to work on new flying boat designs and, in conjunction with a works team, carried out modifications to many United States aircraft for the British Services. Chief among these was the United States flying boat the Consolidated PBY-5 Catalina. Over 300 of these extremely useful aircraft were brought up to Royal Air Force and Fleet Air Arm operational standards.

Typical of the more unusual tasks at Beaumaris was the carrying out of trials on this floatplane version of a Spitfire Mark VB converted by Folland Aircraft Ltd. Obviously performance was significantly reduced and landing on the water was found to be difficult in rough conditions.

A very closely kept secret within the Company during the Second World War was the building of a 16 ft long one-man submersible canoe, code named Sleeping Beauty. Fifteen of these craft, which were capable of diving to a depth of 40 ft, were constructed towards the end of the war for operation in the Far East.

The ruin of Solent Works at West Cowes after the German bombing raid on Cowes in May 1942. The site was cleared and remains clear to this day, apart from a few small buildings adjacent to the road.

Normally referred to as the Short Shetland flying boat, it should properly be referred to as the Short Saro Shetland, since the firms had a combined contract for the machine. The flying boat was designed as a long range, 1,500 miles reconnaissance aircraft capable of carrying bombs, mines and depth charges, with a crew of eleven. Powered by four 2,500 hp Bristol Centaurus VII engines she had an all-up-weight of 130,000 lb. Saunders Roe designed and built the wings and floats and were responsible for the hydrodynamic design of the hull - based on the successful Saro Shrimp. First flown in December 1944, the flying boat was burnt out at her moorings in 1946. With the end of the war no further machines were built.

The civil version of the Shetland was designed to carry forty passengers. Powered by a Centaurus engine uprated to 2,600 hp, it was first flown in 1947. The flying boat was broken up at Belfast in 1951 without carrying a single fare paying passenger.

Three
Saunders Roe Limited 1945-1959

The Second World War had caused the dispersion of much of the Company's work to Addlestone, Edmonton, Beaumaris, Romsey and a multitude of very small out-stations such as garages. The first task at the cessation of the war was, therefore, reorganisation. Aircraft work was primarily at Cowes with an out-station at Eastleigh. The Saunders Shipyard Limited was transferred to Beaumaris, taking over the wartime establishment that had been used for the modification of United States aircraft, and was renamed Saunders Engineering & Shipyard Limited. Later this Company became Saunders-Roe (Anglesey) Limited. Saro Laminated Wood Products Limited continued at their Folly Works on the River Medina, but largely reverted to the production of high quality plywood.

The Company was blessed with teams of expert engineers and skilled workmen who embarked on an incredible variety of successful projects, many of which are described in the ensuing pages.

The Saunders Roe SRA1, originally designated SR44, was nicknamed the 'Squirt' by the shop floor workers. It was the world's first and only jet propelled fighter flying boat. This single seat machine was powered by two 3,850 lb thrust Metropolitan Vickers Beryl axial flow turbojets which gave a top speed of 512 mph (Mach No 0.81). Designed when the team was at Beaumaris, it was assembled at East Cowes. This fighter first flew in August 1947.

This view of the SRA1 shows the clean lines of the hull developed on the A37 'Shrimp' which gave no porpoising problems. Three machines were built, two were lost in accidents and the third is on exhibition in the Southampton Hall of Aviation. Armament consisted of four 20 mm Hispano cannon in the nose and 2,000 lb of bombs could be carried. Unfortunately, with the end of the war there was no operational requirement for the machine.

Design of the huge Saunders Roe SR45 Princess flying boat, the largest metal one ever built, began in 1943. Powered by ten Bristol Proteus gas turbines she was to carry 200 passengers non-stop to New York at a speed of 350 mph at 36,000 ft. The four inboard nacelles contained coupled engines driving contra-rotating propellers. The two outboard nacelles contained a single engine driving a single propeller.

The first Princess hull being assembled in the Columbine hangar in November 1947. The 'double-bubble' hull, with its two passenger decks above the planing hull and its many water-tight compartments can be clearly seen.

The first Princess hull being rolled out of the Columbine hangar on 30 October 1951. In the foreground are two famous flying boat designers: Henry Knowler, the Saunders Roe Chief Designer is on the left with Sir Arthur Gouge, the Chief Designer of Shorts for many years, who at this time was the Chairman of Saunders Roe.

The Princess was ready for launch on 19 August 1952, but a strong beam wind delayed the launch until early the next morning when it took place under floodlights.

The first Princess flight crew. Standing, from left to right: R.B. Stratton (First Engineer), S. Ingle (Powered Flying Control Observer), W.S. Worner (Flight Test Section), G.A.V. Tyson (Chief Test Pilot), J.S. Booth (Co-Pilot), S. Welford (Second Engineer), H. New (Electrician), G. Jones (Flight Test Representative). Front row: H. Palmer (Powered Flying Control Observer), M. Mabey (Radio Observer), A. Walker (Electrician), R.J. Wraith (Electrical Design).

Maintenance of very large aircraft such as the Princess requires a great deal of special equipment and a 'head for heights' among the maintenance crew.

The Princess was a very impressive sight flying low at the Farnborough Air Show in 1952. However, development problems with the Bristol Proteus engines were not overcome in time to convince potential operators of the viability of the machine, and the three aircraft built were all cocooned, one at Cowes and two at Calshot. The last flight of this superb aircraft was in July 1954.

This beautiful jet propelled craft called the Duchess, was the last flying boat designed by Henry Knowler. The year was 1952 and unfortunately she was before her time and never built!

A set of floats were designed and built in 1946 for an Auster Mark VI. This successful one-off modification is seen here floating in the mouth of the River Medina close to the Columbine slipway of the Company.

As part of research into the development of fighter aircraft which could operate from water, an Auster J5G was fitted with hydroskis. Trials in 1954 and 1955 proved that the proposal was completely practical. In spite of this success, backed by extensive theoretical and tank testing work, the Government decided against the concept.

In January 1951 Saunders Roe took over the Cierva Company which was close to their existing facility at Eastleigh. Initially development continued of their W11 Air Horse three rotor helicopter which was powered by a Rolls Royce Merlin engine. After limited ground testing and tethered flying for basic information, the machine was dismantled and stored.

At the time of the Cierva takeover a small two seat single engined helicopter, the W14, had been test flown in 1948. After considerable testing to remove resonance problems and meet service requirements, a production version named the Skeeter was ordered and 78 were built between 1954 and 1960 for the British and German Armies and the German Navy. The production version was powered by a 215 hp Gypsy Major engine.

A Mark 6 Skeeter was equipped as an ambulance and fitted with a Napier NRE 19 rocket booster system. This machine was exhibited at the Farnborough Air Show in 1957. Production of Skeeter aircraft was completed in 1960.

Skeeter helicopters being assembled in the Saunders Roe Eastleigh factory in the 1950s.

The Saunders Roe P531 helicopter prototype was developed directly from the Skeeter. Two prototypes were designed and built in seven months under Ministry of Supply contract. First flown in 1958 with a 425 hp Blackburn-Turbomeca 600 free turbine engine, it was to be called the Sprite. Westland Aircraft Limited took over the Company in 1959 and transferred production to Hayes where 148 were built for the Army (named the Scout), 96 for the Navy (named the Wasp) and a further 45 were exported.

Under contract from the Hiller Company in 1958 their Rotorcycle YROE 1 one man portable helicopter was built at Eastleigh. It was first flown in 1959 with a 43 hp Nelson H63B two stroke engine which gave a maximum speed of 70 mph. Production ceased after ten machines were built, five for the US Marine Corps and five for test and demonstration.

As part of a diversification programme in the late 1950s the Eastleigh division manufactured 250 Medina 7.5 hp outboard engines. A licence to build further engines was sold to J & F Pool Ltd in 1960.

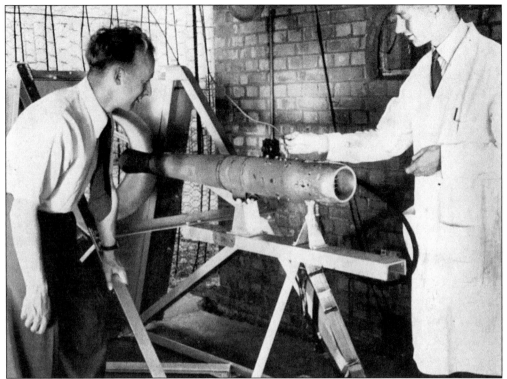

Pulse jet engines were developed at Eastleigh for mounting on the tips of helicopter rotor blades. Two types were designed, the PJ1 with 45 lb thrust - seen here - and the PJ2 with 120 lb thrust. Further development was discontinued in 1959.

After the design team returned to Cowes in 1945 the Saunders Shipyard moved from Edmonton and took over the factory at Beaumaris. The name was changed in 1946 to Saunders Engineering and Shipyard Ltd as light engineering work was required. The Company soon began building double decker buses for London Transport, followed by these buses for Auckland in New Zealand, which were built on a Leyland chassis. Buses were also built at Cowes.

The Royal Navy's first aluminium alloy motor torpedo boats were built at Beaumaris in 1948-9. These were 75 ft long and capable of 42 knots. They were followed in the early 1950s by the Dark class, powered by twin Napier Deltic engines giving a similar speed. This superb action picture shows HMS *Dark Aggressor* firing four 21 inch torpedoes.

Morag Mhor a 72 ft long Bermudian ketch designed by Laurent Giles and Partners was built at Beaumaris in 1953-4. She had the largest all welded aluminium alloy round bilge hull of the period.

Also in the 1950s large quantities of airborne lifeboats were built at Beaumaris. These were 30 ft long and could be carried under Avro Shackleton aircraft. They carried a mast and sails and a Vincent marine engine.

Seven 106 ft long inshore minesweepers were built for the Royal Navy between 1954 and 1956. The first of class ship was HMS *Brenchley*. The first four vessels had mahogany planking with aluminium alloy frames, followed by laminated mahogany frames for subsequent craft. Shown here is HMS *Cradley*, the last of the seven.

In 1954 Saunders Roe received a contract from the Defence Research Board of Canada to design and manufacture a hydrofoil boat based on the ideas of Alexander Graham Bell and E.W. Baldwin. Here the completed craft, called the *Bras d'Or*, is seen at speed off Beaumaris in 1957. This 59 ft long craft powered by two Rolls Royce Griffon 1,750 hp engines was designed at Cowes and built at Beaumaris. In trials it achieved just short of 40 knots.

One of the last of many and varied craft built at Beaumaris before the Westland takeover, was this 41.5 ft long welded aluminium general purpose launch, built there in 1958-9.

The foil design used on *Bras d'Or* was known as the ladder system, as is shown by this photograph of the V-shaped hydrofoils being assembled to the side struts.

Following the success of the SRA1 flying boat fighter the Company continued to work on fighter proposals. Finally a specification was agreed with the Ministry of Supply in 1952 for a single seat short range high altitude interceptor. It was the first mixed power unit fighter to be built. Designated the SR53 it was powered by an Armstrong Siddeley Viper 1,640 lb thrust turbo jet and an 8,000 lb thrust de Havilland Spectre rocket engine. Maximum speed was Mach 2.0 and with the rocket at full thrust it had the astonishing rate of climb of nearly 30,000 ft per minute. First flight was in May 1957.

Three SR53 aircraft were ordered, as this photograph of them being assembled in the Columbine hangar shows. One crashed and its pilot, Squadron Leader John Booth, was killed. No explanation for the accident was ever determined and flying continued with another aircraft until October 1959. The Ministry decided that a bigger payload was needed and the contract for the third aircraft was cancelled.

The SR53 concept with a substantially bigger payload was designated the SR177. This time the turbine engine was a de Havilland Gyron Junior with 14,000 lb thrust, and the rocket was the Spectre uprated to 10,000 lb thrust. Performance increased to Mach 2.35. An order was placed in 1956 for 9 aircraft with cover for up to 27. The Duncan Sandys decision to stop fighter aircraft production in favour of guided missiles caused cancellation of the contract before any aircraft were completed.

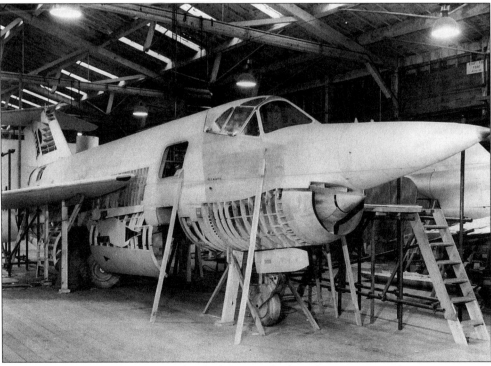

This SR177 mock-up shows more detail of this very high performance aircraft.

The main fuselage bulkheads at the wing attachment points were very complex machinings. At the time of the cancellation of the contract the design was 91 per cent complete and the first aircraft were 50 per cent complete.

The Black Knight atmospheric re-entry test rocket was based on the same technology as that used on the rocket engine of SR53. In the foreground of this picture taken at the launch site in Australia is the standard 32 ft high rocket powered by four Bristol Siddeley Gamma high test peroxide/kerosene engines. The Black Knight could reach an altitude of 600 miles. In the background is a vehicle with a second stage solid fuel Cuckoo rocket to increase the re-entry speed of the test head for the British intercontinental missile Blue Streak.

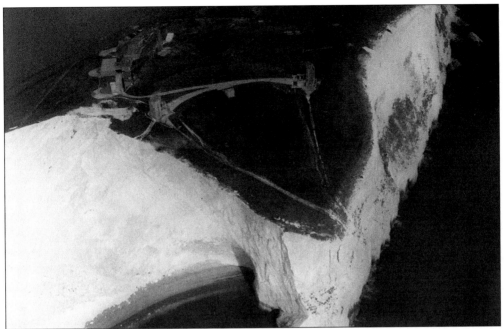

Saunders Roe were responsible for both static testing of Black Knight at this site near the Needles on the Isle of Wight, and the launch facilities at Woomera in Australia. The site on the Isle of Wight was chosen because of the extremely loud noise created by the rockets at full thrust. Two test towers can be seen here, which also shows how the shape of the site dispersed the noise out into the English Channel. The first Black Knight was launched in Australia in September 1958, and the last of 23 successful launches was in November 1965.

Whilst the Company continued its entreprenurial work it never ceased its profitable aircraft sub-contract work, which had commenced in 1908. Typical of these contracts in the 1950s was work for the Vickers aircraft company. This photograph shows the nose section and pressurised control cabin of the Valiant bomber.

The wings for the highly successful Vickers Viscount were produced in quantity at the Company's Eastleigh factory in the 1950s.

Saro Laminated Wood Products Limited at their Folly Works on the River Medina continued to develop their products through the 1950s. This modern plant coated high grade plywood with a hard gloss plastic which they designated Sa R-Ree Z. The plywood was used for high quality partitioning in offices, flats and factories.

A small electronics division was created in the early 1950s to provide complex instrumentation for the Princess programme. The group rapidly expanded and were soon producing complex analogue computers, flight simulators and amplifiers. Computers like the one shown here were produced for customers such as Imperial College and the Ministry of Supply.

The busy Electronics Division workshop is shown here in the mid 1950s. In the foreground is a helicopter drive shaft fitted with a very accurate foil strain gauge invented by the Saunders Roe team to measure torque in the shaft.

Extensive test facilities were provided in the 1950s in the old hospital of the Osborne Royal Naval College. The college hospital buildings in the centre are joined by covered walkways. In the foreground is a test tank in which the Princess models were tested. Structural, mechanical and wind tunnel facilities were contained in other buildings. The Electronics Division is contained in half of the large building at the upper right. Company apprentices received their basic training at this site.

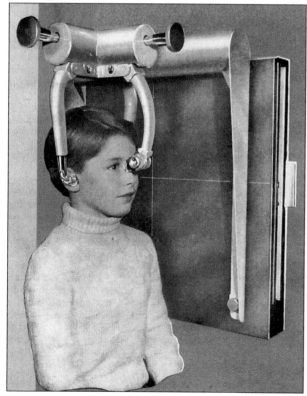

Among many other items manufactured in the late 1950s was this cephalostat to provide accurate positioning of the head for radiography.

Following cancellation of the SR177 fighter programme much effort was expended in seeking alternative work. In 1958 Saunders Roe Structures Limited was set up to take advantage of the Company's rich experience in aluminium alloy structural design. This new company was soon building a variety of civil structures including domed and cylindrical roofs. Here we see a trial assembly of a 350 ft high free standing radio transmission tower constructed of aluminium alloy tubes for British Somaliland in 1959.

Research work on the hovercraft principle invented by Christopher Cockerell began at the Company in 1957. Their favourable report in May 1958 led to the award of a contract to build a manned model, the SRN1, by the National Research and Development Corporation. This photograph shows the testing of a radio controlled model of SRN1 at Osborne Bay on the Isle of Wight.

A contract to build the SRN1 hovercraft was awarded to the Company in October 1958. The craft was completed in May 1959, which was a very short time to design and build such a new concept. The craft was 30 ft long and 24 ft in beam, and was powered by a single 450 hp Alvis Leonides aircraft petrol engine which gave the craft a speed of 30 knots in calm conditions. This photograph shows the craft when demonstrated to the Press on 11 June 1959, just before the takeover of the Company by Westland Aircraft Ltd on 23 July 1959.

Four
Westland Aircraft Limited 1959-1985

In 1959 Westland Aircraft Limited carried out a Government request to merge the nation's helicopter business under their leadership. On 23 July 1959 agreement was reached with the Saunders Roe Board and its principal share holders. Under the agreement the de Havilland Company acquired Saunders Roe (Anglesey) Limited and Saro Laminated Wood Products Limited at Folly on the Isle of Wight; the Westland Company acquired the East Cowes and Eastleigh aircraft and helicopter facilities. Not long after the takeover the helicopter work was transferred to the Fairey factory at Hayes and the Eastleigh factory was sold. The East Cowes design, development and manufacturing facilities were named the Saunders Roe Division of Westland Aircraft Limited.

The development of Christopher Cockerell's hovercraft invention was fully supported by the Westland Aircraft Board in full cooperation with the National Research and Development Corporation. In 1966 the United Kingdom hovercraft interests were combined to form a new company called British Hovercraft Corporation Limited which was 65 per cent owned by Westland, 25 per cent by Vickers and 10 per cent by the NRDC. Christopher Cockerell persuaded the NRDC that the Vosper interest should be licenced to build and they did not join the BHC consortium. Westland bought out the Vickers interest in 1970 and the NRDC interest in 1972, thus making the British Hovercraft Corporation wholly owned by Westland.

Fortunately aeronautical work continued on space launchers Black Knight and Black Arrow and with a number of significant aircraft sub-contracts such as the Britten Norman Islander. This latter work was the foundation for the future when hovercraft work decreased and the Westland Group ran into financial difficulties, to be restructured by Sir John Cuckney in 1985.

Just two days after Westland took over the Company, on the 50th anniversary of the first aircraft crossing by Bleriot, the SRN1 crossed the Channel. She was driven by Lt Cdr Peter Lamb with technologist J.B. Chaplin as engineer and with Christopher Cockerell hanging on grimly to the bow acting as ballast!

In September 1959 SRN1 was demonstrated to the world at the Farnborough Air Show carrying twenty fully armed Marines. With no skirts the controllability of a hovercraft over a smooth runway is at its most difficult, but no problems were experienced.

SRN1 was demonstrated to the Duke of Edinburgh and Eric Mensforth, President of Westland Aircraft Ltd, in December 1959. Christopher Cockerell can be seen in the upper left corner of the photograph which was taken at Osborne Bay. The Duke is accompanied by the Company Chief Test Pilot, Peter Lamb.

The Beach Survey Section of the Naval Intelligence Department commissioned the Company to build this strange amphibious craft known as the WALRUS, an acronym for Water and Land Reconnaissance Unit Survey. A single 50 hp Coventry Climax engine drove the 18.5 ft long craft through two 1 ft diameter contra-rotating helices. Here the craft is being prepared for tethered trials on the Columbine slipway in 1960.

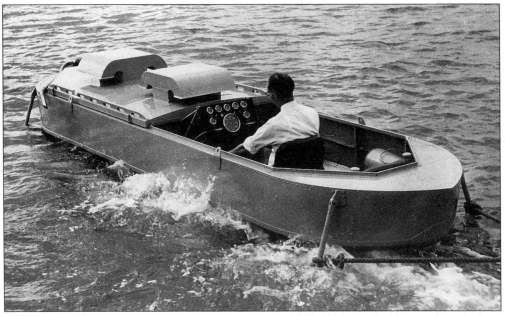

WALRUS undergoing thrust measurement at sea in 1960. Nothing further was heard of the craft after its handover to the Beach Survey Section, possibly because of the advent of amphibious hovercraft.

In late 1959 the National Development Corporation and Westland Aircraft Ltd decided that the hovercraft concept was successful and that they should jointly invest in a craft to carry 59 passengers, to be designated the SRN2. Power was supplied by four Blackburn A129 Nimbus engines giving a total power of 3,260 hp. Each pair of engines drove one lift fan and propellor unit. The photograph shows the craft alongside the SRN1 in its final configuration in 1961.

SRN2 hull under construction in the Columbine hangar in 1961 showing flow diffuser vanes to straighten the flow from the centrifugal fan. These vanes were not used on future craft as the added complexity showed very little increase in aerodynamic efficiency.

SRN2 landing at Appley Beach, Ryde, Isle of Wight, while operating a cross Solent passenger service for Southdown Motor Services Ltd in August 1962. The amphibious capability of the craft was being exploited both at Ryde and at Eastney Beach at Southsea. The technology was proceeding at such a pace at this time that only one SRN2 was built.

Towards the end of 1961 the Ministry of Technology awarded the Company a contract to build a stretched version of the SRN2 for evaluation of the hovercraft principle for military purposes. The craft, the SRN3, was powered by four 900 hp Bristol Siddeley Gnome engines which enabled the craft to carry 92 fully equipped soldiers, or three laden quarter ton trucks and 20 soldiers. Capable of over 70 knots, SRN3 was launched in December 1963.

SRN3 with its side loading ramp deployed, loading a jeep and trailer and fully armed troops in an exercise at Browndown. The craft was operated by the Inter Service Hovercraft Trials Unit which had its operating base at HMS *Daedalus* at Lee-on-Solent.

Typical of the centrifugal fans which provided the air to lift the larger hovercraft is this 12 ft 6 in diameter version. Careful balancing was required to avoid unacceptable vibration in the craft and its transmission system.

After the successful evaluation of hovercraft in a variety of roles for 11 years, the Ministry of Defence decided to check the vulnerability of hovercraft to under-water explosions of large mines. In 1974 SRN3 was subjected to a series of explosions, the last almost right under the craft whilst tethered with the lift system working. Not only did the craft survive the explosion, but it was able to return to base under its own power. The stern of the craft can be seen below the huge plume of the explosion.

The SRN5 was the first hovercraft to be designed from the outset fitted with deep flexible skirts evaluated on the final version of SRN1. The craft, which was nearly 40 ft long and 23 ft in beam, was powered by a single Bristol Siddeley Marine Gnome turbine engine of 960 hp, and could carry 18 passengers or 2 tons of freight. A maximum calm water speed of 66 knots was achieved. The first craft hovered on the Company slipway in April 1964. Fourteen craft were built for operators all over the world, including the Ministry of Defence.

As soon as the SRN5 appeared in service there was a demand for greater carrying capacity. Design of the SRN6 commenced in 1964 to stretch the SRN5 by nearly 10 ft to more than double the payload to thirty-eight passengers. The ninth SRN5 on the production line was the first to be lengthened and took to the water in March 1965.

The SRN5 and SRN6 production line in the East Cowes factory in the mid 1960s. An SRN6 is in the foreground with an SRN5 next to it on the left.

A total of sixty-nine SRN5 and SRN6 craft were built and operated by both civil and military customers. This craft was one of eight built for the Imperial Iranian Navy in 1968 and 1969.

British Rail Hovercraft Limited, Seaspeed, were not content with the stretch of an SRN5 to the 6 and requested a further stretch of 10 ft to increase the passenger capacity to fifty-eight. Two craft were converted in 1972 and to the surprise of many observers, performance was hardly affected and comfort increased.

The final modification of the SRN5/6 series was to develop a craft with a very significant drop in the external noise level. This was achieved on the Mark 6 version by installing two propellors, instead of one, with a much reduced rotational speed. Five of these craft were built in 1982 for the Iraqi Navy.

It was originally the intention to follow the SRN3 with a concept based on a stretch of this craft and a further craft, as it were, alongside. This was to be the SRN4, but the project was delayed to make full use of the deep skirts developed on the SRN1 and N5. The Westland Board authorised design to proceed in 1965 and in 1966, and agreed to merge the Cowes facility with the Vickers Supermarine hovercraft team to form the British Hovercraft Corporation Limited. Contracts were obtained to build two craft for both British Rail Hovercraft Ltd and HoverLloyd Ltd. The first craft, seen here leaving Dover Harbour, began trials in 1967. The four Rolls Royce Marine Proteus engines of 3,400 hp each, drove a variable pitch propellor on a pylon which rotated plus or minus 30 degrees, and a large centrifugal lift fan. The large stern fins could also be rotated for control purposes. The craft carried 254 passengers and 30 standard European cars. One of the SRN4s achieved a maximum speed of 83 knots (96 mph).

The Queen, Lord Louis Mountbatten, Prince Andrew and Viscount Linley descending the steps of the SRN4 with the Westland Chairman, Mr E.C. Wheeldon, during a visit to British Hovercraft Corporation in August 1968.

The Britten Norman Islander nine passenger aircraft powered by two 250 hp Lycoming piston engines, was built by British Hovercraft from 1968 until 1972. A total of 363 aircraft were completed and kits for 29 more were ready for assembly when Fairey SA of Belgium bought Britten Norman and transferred production to Belgium and Romania.

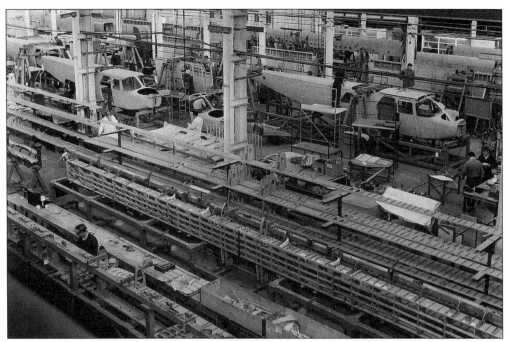

Part of the Islander production line at the Companies East Cowes Falcon Yard in 1970. The yard was bought in 1966 from the old John Samuel White Company when it ceased trading.

A by-product from the Company facility for the manufacture of hovercraft skirts was this wave calming device built for British Petroleum in 1979. The idea was that large mattresses of this type would be moored around the North Sea drilling platforms. Trials were satisfactory, but BP proceeded no further with the project.

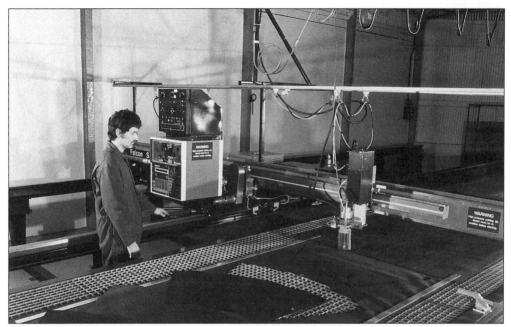

An automatic CAD/CAM facility was developed in the mid 1970s for cutting out parts from rolls of flexible skirt or plastic materials. The cutting head here is a very high pressure water jet, but a laser head could also be used.

Another use for the hovercraft principle was this device built and operated for the Central Electricity Generating Board. Known as the 'on-the-road' heavy transporter, the air cushion, retained by its convoluted skirt, relieved the load of a 300 to 600 ton transformer by 200 tons in order that the transformer could be carried over short span understrength bridges. Power to maintain the cushion was supplied by four Rolls Royce B81 SV petrol engines, delivering a total of 235 hp. Each engine drove a single centrifugal compressor pumping air into the cushion. These transporters were operated by the Company for the CEGB from 1966 to 1993.

Air lubricated pallets were produced in the 1970s to carry loads from 1 to 5 tons. The air could be tapped from the normal air supply provided in most factories, or from a simple compressor. The air was piped under the pallet to flexible diaphragms thus removing most of the friction. Prince Michael of Kent is being easily pushed on a 1 ton pallet in this picture.

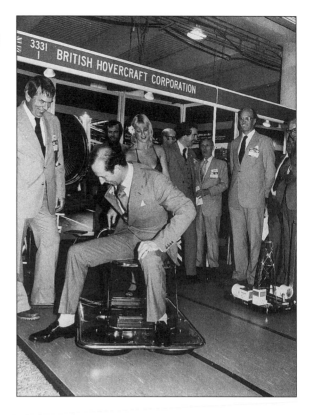

Starting in the mid 1970s, tests of new harbours regarding their effectiveness in calming the sea were carried out in a huge inflated building at the Osborne test facility. This was claimed to be the largest inflatable building in the country. It was wrecked in the 1987 hurricane.

The Company continued to produce load measurement devices utilizing foil strain gauges. The devices varied from small torquemetres to this huge link in the mooring system for Middle East oil companies to ensure that new mooring systems were not over loaded. These load measuring links were produced in the mid 1970s.

The first BH7 was delivered to the Inter Service Hovercraft Unit in 1969. The power unit for this craft was almost identical to one of the four engine, propellor, lift fan units of SRN4. The version shown here is one of six delivered to the Imperial Iranian Navy in the period 1970 to 1975. The machine was used for the logistic support of Iranian military services.

After several years of study of possible British satellite launchers, the Royal Aircraft Establishment decided in favour of a low cost vehicle based on Black Knight to be called Black Arrow. The rocket had three stages; the first was 2 metres in diameter (6 ft 6.7 ins) instead of the 3 ft of Black Knight; the second stage 4 ft 6 ins and the third stage, a Waxwing solid fuel rocket. The 43 ft long rocket was able to put a 320 lb payload into orbit. The successful launch of the satellite *Prospero* took place in October 1971 after only three development launches.

The first stage propulsion unit of Black Arrow comprised eight Rolls Royce Gamma 8 combustion chambers, mounted in pairs on gimballs so that they could be rotated for control purposes. Total thrust provided by these rocket motors was 50,000 lb.

Black Arrow aluminium alloy continuously spot welded fuel tanks in the Falcon Yard at East Cowes in the late 1960s.

Black Arrow first stage on the left and second stage on the right, being finally assembled in the Osborne Works at East Cowes, in the late 1960s.

Black Arrow undergoing full power tests in one of the gantries at the High Down test facility near the Needles on the Isle of Wight, in 1969.

Black Arrow third stage comprising the Waxwing solid fuel rocket (shown in detail upper left), the small separation bay, a development experimental satellite and the assembly crew inside the two folding halves of the nose fairings.

Prospero - Britain's first technological satellite manufactured by Marconi and launched into a near perfect orbit in 1971 by Black Arrow. The project was immediately cancelled by the Government in favour of United States launchers. Black Arrow was Britain's one and only satellite launcher.

The Queen's Award to Industry for Export Achievement was presented to Company Chairman Sir Christopher Hartley in 1975 by Lord Louis Mountbatten.

In 1972 the Company bought a small Isle of Wight Company called Cushioncraft Limited and soon received a contract from the Ministry of Defence for two CC7 machines for the British Army. These small machines were 26 ft long and 15 ft in beam. A single United Aircraft of Canada ST6 engine provided the 510 hp for two 3.5 ft diameter centrifugal fans which provided both lift and propulsion through ducts. This simple but inefficient form of propulsion meant that the top speed was 35 knots. The side bodies outside the central aluminium alloy hull were inflated reinforced rubber bags. Built at Falcon Yard they were delivered in 1972 for exercise Strong Express in Norway.

After nearly two years comprehensive research and development the Company was able to offer British Rail Seaspeed an 80 per cent increase in payload, together with increased performance for their two SRN4 craft. The contract, to lengthen the craft by 55 ft with an entirely new skirt design, was awarded in April 1976. The Proteus engines were retained but uprated from 3,400 hp to 3,800 hp, an increase in power which is rarely used. Designated SRN4 Mark 3, it was soon known as the 'Super Four' because it was an instant success at its launch in April 1978. She is the world's largest hovercraft.

Shortly after the launch of the first 'Super Four' in 1978, Lord Louis Mountbatten, always a hovercraft enthusiast, was taken for a ride in the Solent. He was so pleased with the performance of the craft that he insisted on being the first fare paying passenger. Here he is paying Mr Richard Stanton-Jones, Company Managing Director, a 10p coin for his passage! The Cowes hovercraft team was privileged to receive the 1978 Award for Innovation in Transport by the Worshipful Company of Coach Builders and Harness Makers. Both lengthened craft are still in service some thirty years after their first trials began.

The SRN4 being lengthened in Columbine Yard in 1977. The craft had been constructed of a modular design which made cutting the craft in half and reassembling it with a new centre section a comparitively simple matter. Passenger accommodation was increased from 254 to 418 and the car capacity doubled from 30 to 60. The craft was 185 feet long, 80 ft in beam and had a displacement of 300 tons.

As in the case of Black Knight and Black Arrow, the Company was also responsible for Falstaff launch facilities. The craft with its four large tail fins is shown here being readied for launch. Twelve Falstaffs were built, but as the first six flights were completely successful the remaining six were scrapped. The last launch was in 1979.

Following the cancellation of Black Arrow the Company continued with space work manufacturing payload fairings for a French launcher. In 1972 a Ministry of Defence contract was awarded to develop and produce a space control system test vehicle, code named Falstaff. The vehicle was based on a single solid fuelled rocket 17 ft long and 3 ft in diameter called Stonechat, which was supplied by the Rocket Propulsion Establishment at Westcott. Overall length of the vehicle was some 31 ft and it was capable of launching a 1,200 lb payload to an altitude of 50 miles, giving a long free fall of 120 seconds for testing control systems. Launch of the first rocket was in 1976.

The first BH7 hovercraft was purchased in 1970 by the British Interservices Trials Unit, later to be acquired by the Royal Navy. Many successful trials were carried out with the craft, including a journey to the North Baltic over ice and another along the east coast of the United States. Technical trials proved conclusively the suitability of the craft for mine counter-measures. In 1982 the Company, in partnership with the Royal Navy, Plessey Marine and Racal Positioning Systems, fitted the craft with a complete set of mine hunting systems. What looks like a ship's funnel is the large tube, which carries the underwater sonar system, in its retracted position. Trials at Portland in 1983 were completely successful. Design of a developed BH7 for mine counter-measures began but was discontinued in January 1985 as a result of a Ministry of Defence budget cut.

A major task carried out by the Electronics Division in 1985 was this heavy duty road pavement simulator for the Transport and Road Research Laboratory.

In response to requests for a more economic, quieter hovercraft to replace the SRN6, the Company designed a diesel engined, welded aluminium alloy craft designated AP 1-88 by the Project Office. Commencing in 1980, the Company, the National Research and Development Corporation and the Solent operator, Hovertravel, financed the new craft. The production 100 seat craft was provided with four 428 hp Deutz air cooled diesel engines, two providing propulsion through ducted propellors and two providing lift through six centrifugal fans in back-to-back pairs. Rotatable bow thrusters utilizing air from the lift fans gave control in addition to the rudders in the propeller ducts. The prototype took to the water in July 1982 and later was bought by the US Navy for crew training for their tank landing hovercraft.

AP1-88 ducted propellor installation showing how large the installation has to be to reduce noise. Fourteen craft have been built by the Company, Hovertravel and in Australia.

Five

Westland Aerospace
Limited 1985-1997

When the Westland Group encountered its well publicised financial problems in 1985, the facilities at East Cowes, which had been Saunders Roe Limited, first became the British Hovercraft Corporation Limited and then for a very short time was part of Westland Helicopters and Hovercraft Limited was renamed Westland Aerospace Limited. Since then Westland Aerospace has concentrated on civil aviation programmes, becoming a prime contractor to the world's aircraft manufacturers. In the ensuing years it has acquired a number of other parts of the Westland Group and a Cowes software company called Marex.

The most significant recent change was the 1994 acquisition of the Westland Companies by GKN plc. The Company is now known as GKN Westland Aerospace which, together with GKN Westland Helicopters, GKN Westland Technologies and GKN Defence, form GKN's Aerospace and Special Vehicles Division, one of GKN's three core businesses.

The business operations of GKN Westland are now organised into the following five specialist groups:

1. The largest is the Structures business which designs and manufactures flight critical structures and components from advanced composites and metals for aircraft and helicopters.

2. The Transmissions business designs, develops and produces gearboxes and transmission systems.

3. The Systems business, which produces high technology electro-mechanical measuring systems and specialist computer software packages.

4. Fuel Cells and Flotation Systems manufactures flexible and rigid fuel cells for aircraft and land and marine vehicles, and emergency inflation systems for helicopters.

5. Design Services has the capability to produce high technology designs for major organisations world wide.

The Company now employs 3,200 people and has a turnover in excess of £200 million. No doubt Sam Saunders and Alliott Verdon Roe would be proud of the Company they founded and fostered so many years ago.

The Company has developed Falcon Yard into a high technology composite manufacturing facility. It now has nine autoclaves, the largest is 4.6 m (15 ft) in diameter, 10 m (33 ft) long, has a maximum curing temperature of 400 degrees Centigrade and a maximum pressure of 400 psi. In this photograph an advanced helicopter blade leading edge is being removed from one of the autoclaves.

This large, clean room for laying up advanced composites has an area of 25,000 square feet.

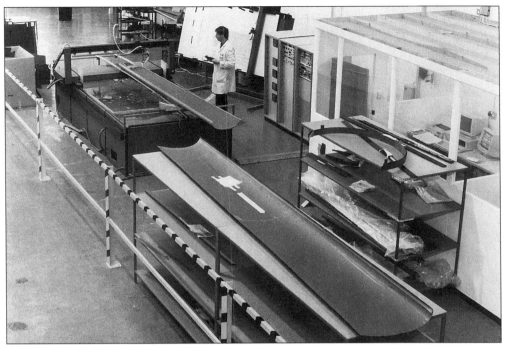

The complete facility has the latest ultrasonic testing equipment to check for faults in components.

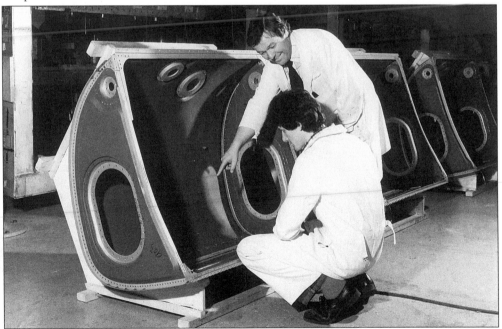

The Company manufactures the long external fuel pods for the Boeing Helicopters CH 47 Chinook helicopter. The first skins were aluminium alloy, but the Company designers persuaded them to change to composite to save weight and cost. In 1987 Westland Aerospace was awarded the prestigious Operation Eagle award by Boeing Helicopters for its response and delivery on the programme.

In the early 1980s the Company established an excellent working relationship with de Havilland of Canada. To date 1,050 nacelles for their Dash 8 series of aircraft have been manufactured. The Company was responsible for design, tooling and manufacture. Nacelles for the Dornier 328, the BAe Jetstream 41, the SAAB 340 and 2000 and the Lockheed Martin C-130J Hercules are now manufactured by the Company.

A number of composite components for the Westland/Agusta EH 101 helicopter have been designed and manufactured at Cowes. This picture shows the glazing structure which is constructed of both kevlar and carbon composites to make the structure both flexible and strong enough to withstand the impact of a 4 lb bird at a speed of 160 knots relative to the helicopter. Work began in the early 1980s and manufacture continues.

In the mid 1980s, to protect Westland Lynx helicopters from heat seeking missiles, the Company developed this high temperature composite diffuser which could be mounted in the exhaust of the helicopter's turbine engine.

The year 1986 saw the delivery of AP1-88 200 *Waban Aki* ('People of the Dawn'), to the Canadian Coastguard. The craft was slightly larger and the engines uprated compared with the standard craft. Still capable of 50 knots, the machine is used for all weather operation on the St Lawrence River. In the spring it is used for ice breaking.

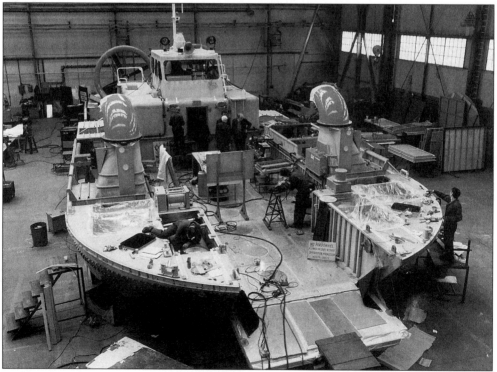

Waban Aki in the final stages of assembly in the Company's Columbine Yard in 1986.

Westland Aerospace were responsible for the design, tooling and manufacture of the inlet duct for the tail mounted engine of the McDonnnell Douglas MD11 jumbo jet. This duct is one of the largest carbon fibre composite structures qualified for a civil aircraft. The contract was awarded in 1990 and some forty ducts have been delivered.

In 1991 the last extension to the Falcon Yard composite facility houses this coordinate measuring machine, the DEA LAMBDA 5711. This machine automatically checks the measurement of components to a high degree of accuracy and is linked directly to the design team computers. Its concrete foundations are 12 ft deep to avoid relative movements of the installation.

The Airbus A 330/340 tyre pressure indication system is supplied by Westland Aerospace. The pressure sensor electronic module fitted to the wheel hub is of similar size to a 20p coin. Seated is Mr Christopher Gustar, Managing Director of Westland Aerospace since 1985.

Electronics is now part of the Aviation Support business of Westland Aerospace and continues to specialise in the design and manufacture of high quality shaft torquemeters, most of which telemeter the strain measurement to the electronic recorder or instrument. This avoids the necessity for slip rings on the shaft. Four typical special installations are shown on this page. Top left: main shaft torque measurement for Her Majesty's warships. Top right: strain measurement of a helicopter rotor head. Bottom left: a flexible panel including strain gauges bonded to the inside of the rotor drive shaft of the Bell V22 Osprey tilt rotor aircraft. Bottom right: the very small drive shaft of a current Formula 1 racing car.

The high technology flexible and inflatable structures business of Westland Aerospace still operates in Portsmouth under the management title of FPT Industries Ltd. Top left: rugged air portable fuel cells. Top right: emergency inflation systems. Bottom left: rotationally moulded containers. Bottom right: flexible fuel cells.

Opposite: In addition to the structures facility at East Cowes, Westland Aerospace has a high quality aluminium alloy aircraft construction works at Yeovil. This rear fuselage for SAAB 2000 is constructed there, together with doors, complete with their appropriate mechanisms for Global Express, Dornier 328 and the de Havilland Dash 8.

The Transmissions group of Westland Aerospace manufactures high quality gearboxes and shafts for civil and military aeroengines and helicopters. This facility is located at Yeovil in Somerset.

The latest AP1-88 the Dash 400 is being built in Canada for Westland Aerospace. The craft was designed at East Cowes and the build is being supervised by the Company engineers. Completion is expected in late 1997 or early in 1998. Two craft are shown here in the Canadian factory.

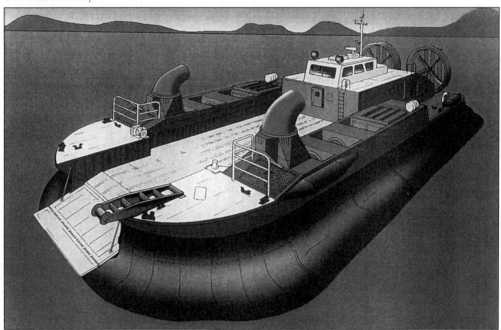

An artist's impression of the AP1-88 Dash 400 for the Canadian Coastguard which will join *Waban Aki* on the St Lawrence estuary. The craft is 4 metres longer and nearly 1 metre wider than *Waban Aki*, and has four Caterpillar 3412TTA diesel engines rated at 671 kw each, compared with 380 kw each for *Waban Aki*.

The Company's 1997 high technology composite facility at Falcon Yard half a mile up the River Medina from the Columbine Yard. All the white roofed buildings are part of the facility which is on the far side of the river in this picture. Half of the buildings have been constructed and the other half completely modernised since this old John Samuel White shipyard was purchased in 1966.

The GKN Westland Aerospace East Cowes facility as it is in 1997. All the factory buildings in this picture belong to the Company. Most of them existed in the Saunders Roe days. The old residence in the right foreground, known as Seaholme, houses the Company directors. The Union Jack on the Columbine door was originally painted to celebrate the Queen's Silver Jubilee. This building, erected by Saunders Roe in 1935, occupies the site taken over by Samuel Saunders in 1906.

Acknowledgements

The author is indebted to his old Company, GKN Westland Aerospace for their unrestricted access to their archive collection. In particular their Public Relations Manager, Mr A.J. Roden, was extremely helpful and always accessible. My wife Jean produced the text and captions on her word processor and was always ready with helpful suggestions for improvements.

The photographs in this volume were obtained from the GKN Westland Aerospace archives. Whilst the author is fully aware that their origin is often unknown it can be assumed that the old established photographic firm of Beken of Cowes Ltd must have supplied many of the photographs. It is known that some have come from the Kirk Collection of Paul Ebbatson of East Cowes, and others from the Imperial War Museum, the Royal Marine Museum and the Isle of Wight County Marine Museum at Cowes. Many have come from individuals too numerous to mention. The author apologises for any inadvertent lack of courtesy in acknowledging any individual or organisation.

Further Reading

From Sea to Air: The Heritage of Sam Saunders. A.E. Tagg and R.L. Wheeler.
Published by Cross Publishing, Walpen Manor, Chale, Isle of Wight. ISBN 0 9509 7393 9

From River to Sea: The Marine Heritage of Sam Saunders. Raymond L. Wheeler.
Published by Cross Publishing, Walpen Manor, Chale, Isle of Wight ISBN 1 8732 9505 7.